DURHAM UNIVERSITY'S ORIENTAL MUSEUM MUMMIES

B. A. ATKINSON

Typeset in Baskerville

Editing, design, typesetting and publishing by UK Book Publishing

www.ukbookpublishing.com

ISBN: 978-1-912183-83-8

Book Cover: Transitional form Ba/Mummy mask EG733

Back Page: Canopic Jars

Note: All Durham mummy images are by kind permission of Durham University Oriental Museum

CONTENTS

IMAGES

BIRDS

SNAKES

FOREWORD

Rachel Barclay, *Curator, Oriental Museum, Durham University*

O ne of the great pleasures of being a museum curator is getting to know the researchers who study the collections. At the Oriental Museum we are lucky enough to care for a wonderfully diverse collection, which attracts scholars from across the globe who have an equally diverse range of interests. It is wonderful to work with these people as they progress from their initial ideas, through the ups and downs of research, toward publication. This can often take many years of hard work and dedication.

It has been a particular pleasure to get to know Barbara over the years she has been visiting the Oriental Museum and researching the collections. Anyone who has met Barbara cannot doubt her passion for ancient Egypt, and particularly for mummies and mummification. An afternoon spent in the archives or stores with Barbara is always guaranteed to leave me smiling, so infectious is her enthusiasm.

I know that this book is the result of a huge amount of commitment. There have been more than a few ups and downs along the road to publication but Barbara was never going to let anything get in the way of achieving this dream. I hope readers will gain as much happiness from reading this book as I know Barbara has obtained from writing it.

ACKNOWLEDGEMENTS

This book could not have been written without the help of various museum curators, archaeologists, Egyptologists and photographers, regarding the Unknown Lady, also known as 'the Mummy with Prosthetic Hand'; the Teenage Boy; Baby and various animal mummies at the Durham Oriental Museum, and I would therefore like to thank them accordingly.

Firstly, many thanks to Mrs. Rachel Barclay, Curator of Durham University Oriental Museum, for all her help and patience, allowing me access to information held at the museum, and it is with enormous gratitude that I thank her for giving me permission to use images of the museum's mummies in this book. Rachel's help via e-mail and personal meetings have been invaluable. Thanks must also go to Sydney Thompson Chapman BA, MPhil, PhD, Curator of Penrith & Eden Museum, who kindly e-mailed me information on the mummy's known origins and advising me to contact Manchester Museum to whom he gave permission to take DNA samples for an Egyptology project.

A big thanks to Dr. Karen Exell, former Curator of Egypt and the Sudan, The Manchester Museum, University of Manchester for putting me in contact with Professor Rosalie David who conducted Bio-medical research on the unknown lady. Professor David in turn passed me to Dr. Jacky Finch who studied the mummy and wrote a thesis regarding her findings. Jacky kindly permitted me access to her thesis, from which I gained further information.

Last but not least, I thank my brother Mr. Graham W. Edwards for allowing me to use his photograph of the Peruvian mummy, and the information he was given by his guide in Peru.

I dedicate this book to my wonderful husband John and our two daughters Angela Marie and Julie Anne.

CHAPTER ONE

Introduction and background

The Oriental Museum in Durham is part of the University of Durham and holds a range of artefacts from around the world, displaying objects from China, Japan, India and Egypt. The museum is well worth a day out, but should your stay in the area be longer than a day, then take in the surrounding area and the famous Durham Cathedral.

There are a number of mummies which are housed in the Museum including animals, birds, reptiles and humans, many of which are on display, others 'resting' in the vaults until it is their turn to be displayed. The most famous of the Egyptian artefacts is the mummy of the Unknown Lady, which it has been said though not confirmed, was lent by Darlington Council to a local cinema to stand in the foyer as a promotion for the film in which Boris Karloff starred as the lead character in Karl Freund's 1932 film 'The Mummy'.

Along with the Unknown Lady, I shall briefly discuss a few other mummified artefacts from the collection, one of which is that of a baby held safe and secure in the 'vaults'.

The word 'mummy', in this respect, originates from the Arab/Persian word 'mummiya', a black tar like substance, also known as bitumen, which ancient Egyptians used to coat the body of the deceased. Around the 4th dynasty, the Egyptians mastered the technique of mummification leading to modern day embalming, though by the late Egyptian period, the techniques varied, changing significantly, until the process eventually ceased.

Mummies are not purely Egyptian; they have been discovered worldwide: for instance in Denmark the 'Skrydstrup mummy' was discovered in a Danish grave mound; Italy produced mummified monks from the Palermo's Capuchin Monastery. Other cultures including Greenland, Mexico, United States of America, Australia and Peru have all unearthed various bodies in a state of 'natural' mummification brought on by diverse meteorological elements. The Peruvian mummy is shown in situ and is possibly a shaman. The material hanging on the wall is human hair, which was alleged to be uncut during the person's lifetime, and the burial is 'egg shaped', as the Peruvians held the opinion that they would hatch out of the egg at their rebirth. This was told to my brother Mr. Graham W. Edwards by his guide whilst he was in Peru. Note too that within the confines of the deep pit tomb are various bones, skulls and pots.

Peruvian Mummy
Courtesy of Mr. Graham W. Edwards

Early mummies were formed mainly due to earthly conditions, when the Egyptians buried their dead straight into the ground. They were unaware that the elements, such as hot sun and sand, would cause dehydration inducing preservation of the body, which in turn triggered natural mummification. Early discoveries include corpses with virtually every body part intact including nails, hair and teeth. Prior to 3,400BC, everyone from the poor to the king were buried in pit graves and brick tombs, along with a few personal possessions.

One very ancient Egyptian 'natural' mummy is known by the name 'Ginger' due to the colour of his hair. He was discovered in the desert sands along with some bowls dating to c.3,400BC and is now housed in the British Museum.

It is worth noting that when mummification is mentioned, it is Egypt which springs to most people's minds, with a myth surrounding mummies in general. Despite media portrayal, they do not return to wreak revenge on grave robbers, Egyptologists or archaeologists. This idea was instigated by the media believing a death curse protected the tomb of pharaoh Tutankhamun. This was due to a couple of incidents which occurred when the tomb was entered by the two leading protagonists, Howard Carter and Lord Carnarvon.

- A cobra ate Howard Carter's canary (cobras were the pharaoh's protectors)
- Lord Carnarvon died due to a mosquito bite becoming infected when he cut himself whilst shaving.

A shrine of Anubis discovered in the king's tomb was inscribed with the words *"It is I who hinder the sand from choking the secret chamber. I am for the protection of the deceased,"* whilst a reporter added the words – *"and I will kill all those who cross this threshold into the sacred precincts of the Royal King who lives forever"*. All of this served to escalate rumours and was quickly adopted and portrayed by authors and film makers. This of course helped to boost the sale of the film and books, a great money earner.

However, Howard Carter who opened the tomb with Lord Carnarvon died naturally at approximately 65 years old, but the film industry made a fortune on producing various mummy films, encouraging belief in the 'curse of the pharaohs'. The most recent films being 'The Mummy' and 'The Mummy Returns' starring Brendan Fraser and Rachel Weisz.

The following chapters deal with the origins of mummification, the process and religion, in order for the reader to understand the mystery surrounding mummies and the artefacts held in the Oriental Museum.

CHAPTER TWO

Preparation and Mummification of the Body

ORIGINS OF MUMMIFICATION

Ancient Egyptians preferred mummification to standard burial or cremation due to their belief in life after death and preservation of the body. Animals including crocodiles, cats and birds were also mummified and often placed in the tomb with their owners. Immortality was paramount; they longed to live in eternity and be remembered forever. The mummification process, along with religious enactments, specifically speaking the name of the deceased, was meant to ensure this.

Artificial preservation of the body originated with Osiris, God of the underworld, judge of the dead, brother/husband of Isis and father of Horus. According to legend, Osiris was murdered by his brother Seth, dismembered and distributed throughout Egypt. Isis and her sister Nephthys searched for his body parts and on gathering them, they re-assembled his body and Anubis embalmed him. Once completely bandaged he therefore formed the first 'mummy.'

Various attempts at ensuring the body remained intact involved placing the deceased on a bed of twigs and/or encasing the corpse in a coffin made of twigs. Following this, they attempted to place the cadaver in a wooden coffin in a tomb, although these burials were also unsuccessful as the corpses decayed. Further attempts at preservation failed, including bandaging the body, with subsequent attempts made which involved coating the linen in resin, wrapping it around the corpse and encasing the body in plaster, which was shaped to the bodily figure. In order for the deceased to be recognised in the underworld, a plaster face was painted with the features of the deceased. However, once again the body rotted and only the cast survived, albeit not always intact. The process continued to be developed and eventually success was obtained around the fourth dynasty. What the early attempts lacked was the understanding of the rotting process, which began with the internal organs. Once they were removed and the body desiccated, then the procedure worked.

The finest preserved specimens that have been discovered belong mostly to the high upper classes, as only they could afford the best and most expensive treatment, which was more likely to obtain the desired effect – eternal preservation. Included in this form of mummification were Queen Hatshepsut, Pharaohs Ramesses II, Ramesses III and of course Tutankhamun. There are others but too many to mention here. As we will see, the Oriental museum mummies, which are not royal, are also well-preserved specimens.

There were three types of known mummification, completion taking around 70 days from death to interment. Usually there were 15 days for cleaning and purifying the body, 40 days' drying period and 15 days for bandaging. All processes used natron, a salt comprising four types of sodium – carbonate, bicarbonate, chloride and sulphate – which dried out the corpse by removing bodily fluids, the cause of decomposition.

The most expensive option was exclusively reserved for pharaohs and nobles. This included the removal of the internal organs, namely the liver, lungs, stomach and intestines. The brain was removed prior to the organs, generally via the nostrils using a tool similar to a long crochet hook. This broke through the sphenoid and ethmoid bones into the cranial cavity to reach and remove the brain. The hook was moved vigorously around to scramble the brain which, when pliable, was drawn out. On occasion, a hole was made in the base of the skull and the grey matter removed from that area. The skull cavity was then often filled with a resin coated cloth. The Egyptians did not think the brain served a purpose in the afterlife and there is speculation as to whether the brain was thrown away or taken with the body for burial. The heart which was believed to be the 'thinking organ', was left in-situ.

One papyrus states there are 11 operations during embalming, each having a specific religious purpose to transform the deceased into a mummy and immortality as a God (if you were a pharaoh). The elite and lower classes, regardless of which procedure they could afford, were merely hoping to attain immortality and live in the 'field of reeds'.

AN EXPENSIVE PROCEDURE

Following brain removal, the body was taken to the *IBW (place of purification),* for desiccation, and the internal organs were treated for preservation, wrapped and placed in canopic jars which were guarded over by the four sons of Horus, which in turn were protected by four Goddesses relating to the four compass points.

The jackal headed Duamutef protected the stomach and was in turn protected by Neith, Goddess of the East

The falcon headed Qebehsenuef was protector of the intestines and he was protected by Serket, Goddess of the West

Baboon headed Hapi looked after the lungs and his protector was the Northern Goddess Nephthys

Lastly, human headed Imsety was responsible for the liver and was protected by Isis, Goddess of the South

Duamutef EG1200

Qebehsenuef EG1190

Hapi EG1194

Imsety EG1195

Once the body had been cleansed using spices, wines and chemicals, priests covered the corpse in dry natron until it was fully desiccated. It was then taken to the **PER NEFER** (house of beauty) for the final preparation, where it would be re-washed and bandaged. Between layers, the embalmers often, but not always, placed protective amulets: Ankh for life, djed pillar for strength and stability, scarab indicating rebirth, heart scarab to protect the heart and a golden Ba Bird placed on the chest to assist the soul to return to the body each night. Many other amulets used to ward off evil would be wrapped or placed next to the body. When bandaging was complete, the finished mummy would be returned to the family and placed in the coffin ready for burial. In the case of the pharaoh, he would be encased in an anthropoid coffin, which was placed inside another coffin, which in turn would be interred in a graphite sarcophagus in his tomb.

Ankh EG5873

Djed pillar EG3660

Scarab EG3195

Ba Bird EG4431

SECONDARY MUMMIFICATION

The lower priced process used by middle class citizens involved injecting cedar oil into the back passage or abdomen, then plugging the anal cavity. The corpse is then covered in natron to dry out and when complete the plug is removed for the internal organs to drain away in liquid form. This prevented them being retained in canopic jars and the body was returned to the family for burial.

BASIC PREPARATION

The cheapest method, which was all the lower classes could afford, involved cleaning the body internally with purge (internal cleanser), desiccation and returning the body to family.

MUMMIFICATION PROFESSIONALS

The following professions were involved in the full mummification of a body:

The Cutter made the incision in the left side to remove the organs. Although the preservation of the body was essential in ancient Egypt, the cutter was low in society as this was considered unclean.

The Scribe ensured the cutter completed the process correctly.

The Embalmer, being of the priesthood and wearing the jackal headed mask of Anubis, removed the organs and mummified the deceased. He was also known as 'overseer of the mysteries (hery-seshta)'. His assistant was known as 'seal-bearer of the God (hetemw-netjer)', whilst the 'Lector priest (hery-heb)' read the spells. These three people oversaw the work of the 'bandagers (wetyw)', who often also removed the organs.

Woodworkers and Masons would be employed in the making of the coffins and sarcophagi, and ensured the stone cutting, carving and shaping was to the required dimensions. The texts had to be word perfect so that the soul could travel safely through the underworld, ensuring constant protection from evil. Artists and scribes would paint or carve the required words or images, whether it was a standard request or fit for a pharaoh with elaborate scenes.

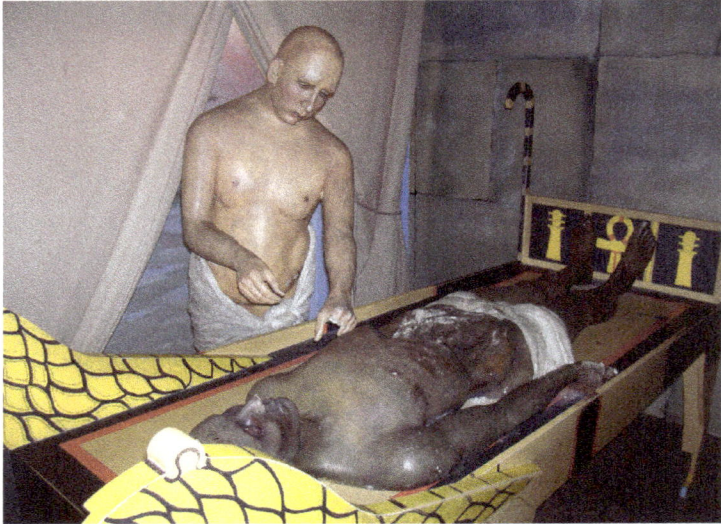

The cutter
By kind permission of Steve at http://newcastlephotos.blogspot.com

CHAPTER THREE

Religion

I n order to gain eternal life, the ancient Egyptians believed the first step was to be mummified in the manner of Osiris.

Religion touched every aspect of Egyptian life, and great care was taken to honour the Gods at all times, even in death. Early burials included burying personal and household goods with the corpse and sometimes sacrificing servants to help with work in the afterlife. Eventually these human sacrifices were replaced with shabti, small mummy shaped statuettes, often inscribed with Chapter VI from the Book of the Dead, stating that in the name of the deceased, the shabti could be called upon to do the work required. This section is taken from the Papyrus of Ani:

> *"the overseer Osiris Ani, triumphant. Hail **shabti** figure this, if be decreed [Osiris], if he be adjudged, to do labours any [which] are to be done in the underworld, ... I will work, verily I am here [when thou] callest there."*

Although I have chosen to quote from the papyrus of Ani, individuals chose their own wording and requests for their papyri to see them through the underworld, should they desire to have one, or if they could afford one.

During the process of mummification magical spells and prayers were recited for the deceased, to hopefully ensure a safe journey to their afterlife. Prior to the body being interred a final rite was conducted. This was known as the Opening of the Mouth ceremony, usually performed by a ritual priest, who used various implements including an adze to touch each part of the face in order to restore speech, sight, hearing and smell in the hereafter.

On his or her travels to the next life, the deceased had to pass the final test in the Hall of Judgement. This was the Weighing of the Heart ceremony; it was so feared that prayers, magic spells and verses from the Book of the Dead were written on tomb walls, coffins, papyrus and other sources to help the deceased pass the test. The requirement was that the deceased's heart would not weigh heavier than the feather of Ma'at, the Goddess of truth and justice. Should the heart weigh heavy, Ammut, a fearful underworld animal with the head of a crocodile, lion's torso and a hippopotamus's rear end, would eat it. This would render the deceased to a second death, unable to enter eternity and be a ghost for ever. When the heart weighed light or the same as Ma'at's feather, then this would be recorded by Thoth and the person travelled on to the 'field of reeds', their concept of heaven.

As previously stated, protective amulets were often placed within the bandages and placed in the coffin, whilst Gods and Goddesses were depicted on the coffins alongside prayers and spells known as the coffin and pyramid texts. There were, on occasions, texts inscribed onto the bandages as we will see later.

In order for the departed to be recognised in the afterlife, there were a few requirements. A funerary mask painted in the likeness of the person was made and placed over the face. Sometimes the masks would be made of cartonnage, comprising linen or papyrus, built up in stripped layers, formed to the shape of the deceased's face. This was held together with plaster and linen, which acts in a similar fashion to papier-mache when moulded and set. Once hardened the artists then completed the process by painting the features onto the surface. Anthropoid coffins also depicted the face, the most famous mask and coffin being that of Tutankhamun, which was made of Gold. Other features adorning the coffin and sarcophagi were eyes painted on both sides so the deceased could see out; false doors for the spirit to come and go; and of vital importance, their name. It was essential that the person's name be known and spoken for them to continue living in the afterlife. Family and friends would speak their name and leave offerings at the tomb to be enjoyed by their loved one. Many people still do this today by leaving flowers at a grave and having headstones or plaques placed in the cemetery in remembrance of the person.

Elements which were crucial for the dead to travel through eternity were the following:

- *Ka*, a person's life force, their sustenance
- *Ba*, linked to the physical body
- *Akh*, the Ka and Ba joined together, the form the deceased takes to travel through the underworld
- *Shadow*, a person's protection
- *Name*, given at birth and required for existence and required for identity in eternity.

As religion was fundamental to Egyptian society, life and death were essentially one and the same, hence the sacred amulets, magical writings on coffins and in tombs along with the need for the body and organs to be preserved for use in the spirit world.

CHAPTER FOUR

Durham Oriental Museum Mummies

UNKNOWN LADY – DUROM.1999.32

This mummy was originally believed to be in the Egyptian Boulaq Museum, which is today's Cairo Museum. Her provenance was possibly from Akhmim (known to the ancient Egyptians as Ipu or Khentmin), on the east bank of the Nile in upper Egypt, although her origin is not conclusive. It has been suggested that she may have been found by Gaston Maspero, Director of the then Boulaq museum on his discovery c.1880sAD, of a Ptolemaic era cemetery in Akhmim. Characteristically the preservation and decoration method used on the mummy and coffin suggests she could be from the Ptolemaic period c.250BC. Due to being devoid of name or title on the casing, as these have sadly been worn away with time, she is referred to as 'the unknown lady' or the 'mummy with the prosthetic hand'.

From the Boulaq museum, the mummy we presume was sold to a private collector and was later donated to the Penrith Public Library and Eden Museum on June 19th 1888, by a Miss Wilson from Penrith. The mummy then subsequently became part of the meso-oriental and oriental antiquities collection. She has been to other various 'homes', being transported from Penrith to Darlington Library and Museum in the 1930s, where, as I previously mentioned, the council may have used her to publicise 'The Mummy' in which Boris Karloff starred. Following on from Darlington she was initially on loan in 1960 to Durham University Oriental Museum, and from here Rachel Barclay, Curator of the Museum, advises that Manchester Museum borrowed her for DNA and Egyptology study purposes. She is now on permanent display in the Thacker Gallery in the University of Durham Oriental Museum, following the loan being converted into a formal transfer in 1999. Professor Thacker was a founding father and first director of the Museum and the gallery is named in his honour.

There have been various tests on the unknown lady, with some results pointing to her being a male priest, others that the sex is female, though I shall refer to the mummy as female. The results of x-rays, which were taken in 1964, initially reported her to be male. This could be attested by an inscription which gives the title 'priest' on the foot of the coffin. *'Professor Thacker, the first Director of the School of Oriental Studies, is the one who is said to have read priest. I have to say that I am not even convinced about the 'hm', the 'ntr' for God is the only really visible hieroglyph, so I would be much less definite about this[1].'* Though this is not conclusive evidence of the mummy being a man, as the female 't' making the word 'priestess' may have been obliterated due to damage.

Examinations of the mummy have suggested that it is that of a slightly built male. There are no obvious fractures, and the whole human form appears intact bar the left hand. Osteoarthritis is in evidence in the lumbar vertebrae area and linen packing has been discovered within the body. The arms are crossed with the right hand on the left shoulder. The left hand was possibly amputated during the lifetime, or the person

---

1.   As told by Mrs. Rachel Barclay, Curator of the University of Durham Oriental Museum

was born with a defective limb. The pelvic area is shown to be empty, the hips are intact with normal joints and the feet are normal, though the legs show Harris lines, which suggests bone development was incomplete. This could possibly have been caused by dietary deficiency.

From further and later examinations, there are suggestions that the mummy could be female, due to the shape of the pelvic area. From my research[2] and personal observations of the artefact, I feel that the mummy, through investigation along with various opinions of others, indicate this to be the case. The face mask also leads me to believe this, as it appears to have primarily feminine features.

Among the results of the examinations, the brain was shown to have been removed (excerebration), via the nose, following which resin had been poured into the skull, which was a later mummification procedure; another indication that she was possibly from the Ptolemaic era. Her teeth were found to be well worn with the mouth containing abscesses. The wearing down of the teeth could possibly be attributed to the ancient Egyptian diet, where bread was made from ground emmer wheat. During the grinding process, sand and grit entered the mixture, therefore when eaten would have affected the tooth enamel. This, accompanied by poor dental hygiene, resulted in infection, which in turn caused abscesses. Her rib cage had suffered no damage during evisceration (removal of the internal organs), and the resulting cavity contained large resin impregnated bandages.

She was cut open to remove the artificial arm which was crossed over her chest. This caused dreadful damage to her torso, as a tenon saw was used to remove the limb, resulting in a long gash across her upper body,

---

2   Research via-emails, Durham Oriental Museum archives, Dr. Jacqueline F. Finch's Thesis – "Prosthesis or Restoration? A Detailed Study of the Left Forearm of Durham Mummy DUROM 1999.32.1"

plus diagonal incisions both left and right from the shoulders. Her arm it is now thought was not amputated, but malformed during pregnancy, as the growth ended just above the wrist. The prosthetic hand was made to fit from the end of the stump.

Torso damage

Further tests were carried out in 1965, 1995 and 2004, which included x-ray tomography (C.T. scan), endoscopy to remove tissue samples and a small sample from the right side for investigation. These are far better ways of examining artefacts than intrusive operations which were carried out in years gone by. These later tests attest previous findings of arthritis, malnutrition, dental abscesses and stunted growth of the upper limb. They also discovered she suffered from knee joint narrowing, kidney and/or gall stones, a broken toe, slipped disc and malnutrition as a child.

The aforementioned prosthetic hand was made of linen and fitted at mummification in order for her to be intact in the afterlife. In 1965 the prosthesis was taken away for research and this now rests at the side of her body as she is too fragile for refitting.

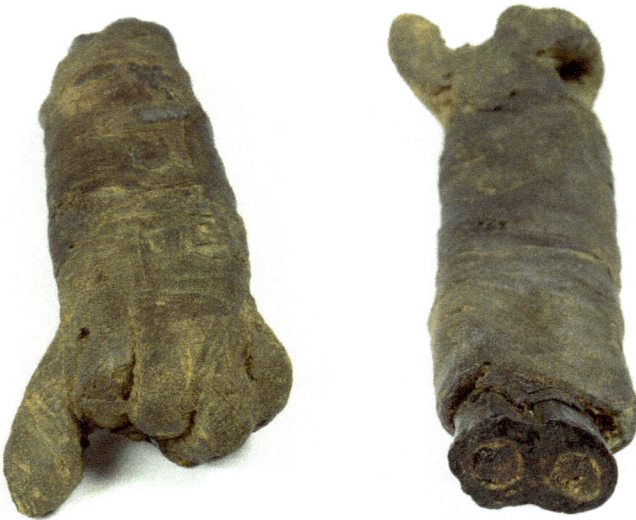

Prosthetic hand

Although the mummification and coffin indicate she was a well to do woman, her deformity and malnutrition suggests she was possibly born into a poorer family. It is estimated she lived to approximately fifty-sixty years old, a considerable age for an ancient Egyptian and she would have been considered a very old woman. Out of respect, her wrappings have never been fully removed, and it appears there were no amulets showing on the x-rays that were taken, therefore Rachel states *"the C.T. scan has been misplaced so we can't check that."* Research is ongoing regarding the unknown lady, and hopefully one day her name may be revealed, allowing her the privileges of the afterlife which she would have wanted.

The intrusive investigations of the past are not allowed today; all investigations are carefully monitored using modern non-intrusive technology. As of April 2011, the Akhmim Mummy Studies Consortium: Research discussion: concluded – the mummy was possibly of the female gender.

THE MUMMY AND HER COFFIN

On the exterior of the coffin lid there is quite a lot of damage, with the wood splitting down the side, and from toe to chest up and across the top. Even though the decoration is mainly faded, there are sections on the upper body which depict Gods in horizontal rows separated by red, black and green squares. The head section colours are extremely dull, yet retain a quality of Egyptian art, and in typical style she is shown wearing the tripartite wig painted black with the sun disc on the forehead. Holding this sun disc in its claws from the back of the head is a winged scarab, with the wings coming down both sides of the wig. Her eyes are painted in the 'elongated' style, the corners ending near the ears and her lips, now dulled, would once have been bright red. Curiously, the face is darker in nature, which is unusual for a female, as women were painted in a lighter hue than their male counterparts. The darkness, though, could be attributed to possible weathering, ageing of the object, water and atmospheric conditions, as opposed to the former speculation that this mummy could have been male. Only the finding of a name and title would settle this debate.

Outside Lid Face and chest

Winged scarab on top of head

Outside coffin lid

INNER COFFIN AND MUMMY

Original photographs show the lady's arm was initially placed across the chest in her inner coffin. Now the prosthesis lies at her side, as to attempt to re-fix it in place could cause further damage.

*Unknown lady in coffin with hand over chest prior
to repositioning at the side of the body*

She is laid to rest in the beautifully decorated outside coffin, measuring 165cm long – approximately 5ft 4ins, therefore she will be smaller again as her body is encased in the inner coffin complete with cartonnage face mask, breastplate, hip to knee panel and foot panel all decorated in blue, red, green, black and white paint on what appears to be a very faded yellow background. Colours in ancient Egypt were of great significance – they had more implication than aesthetic value or mere adornment.

- Green (wadi) represented regrowth, vegetation and new life
- Red (desher) indicated life and victory
- White (hedj/shesep) was purity and omnipotence
- Black (kem) had a few and opposing meanings: death and night, resurrection, fertility and life
- Egyptian Blue (irtiu/sbedj) was related to the sky and water, life and rebirth
- Yellow (khanet/kenit) meant imperishable, eternal and indestructible.

When we analyse these colours and hues in the decoration of funerary equipment, we can understand the reasoning behind their usage. The red and green could symbolise her victory over death along with the yellow giving her eternal life, whilst the black fights against the blue of rebirth, even though itself represents resurrection and life. Finally, the white of supreme power accompanies the yellow of indestructibility, possibly depicting the battle over life and death had been won, and the deceased would live in eternity as they had on Earth. In Egyptian folklore, there is an on-going battle for achieving life in the 'field of reeds', until one has undergone the final test of the Weighing of the Heart ceremony in the Hall of Justice before Osiris, God of the Underworld.

The base of the outer wooden coffin is also decorated, but only with a snake on the left and right sections. They are painted in white with a red 'ladder' pattern running up the centre of their bodies. The single eye is black on a head which faces the deceased, and both snakes wear the white crown of upper Egypt, representing the royal uraeus snake of protection.

Protective snake on side of coffin

FACIAL MASK

Her burial mask unfortunately contains a few damaged sections, but still retains the shape to cover her head, top of the shoulders and sternum. As is the norm, it is in the form of a tripartite wig, a common style for elite facial adornment. The decoration consists of a red and white check pattern across the crown, which is broken up due to a gaping hole to the left, which when outwardly repaired and placed over the mummy's face, revealed the skull below the remaining broken cartonnage.

Just above the red sun disc on the forehead and within a thin white ring are the remnants of a protective winged scarab, replicating the outer coffin mask. These are painted onto the faded blue 'fringe', which drapes down over each shoulder, ending in a white, red and black border. This hairstyle frames a partially damaged gold face, which stares back from black eyes outlined in the classic Egyptian style and adorned with thick black eyebrows.

Faces are painted gold or covered in gold leaf as this is the colour of the skin of the Gods, and individuals were hoping to gain deity status in the afterlife, or at the very least be in the favour of the Gods. Sadly the nose and mouth are also damaged, but there is the vestige of a smile, and on her neck and upper chest is the distinctive traditional broad collar decorated in red, white, black and blue patterns. The sides of the mask are painted with a red and white edging which completes the décor. These colours are brighter than the rest of her adornment, apart from the breastplate which has managed in parts to have stood the test of time, appearing to have been painted only yesterday.

Facial mask prior
to restoration

After basic restoration

BREASTPLATE

On the breastplate we find a beautifully divided layout comprising three sections enclosed in a blocked edging, all on a red background, the original bright colours faded. The major figures are depictions of Horus painted in black and white, topped with a yellow washed-out sun disc, which now appears to have a creamy hue. In this form, Horus is known as Re-Horakhty – Re who is Horus of the two horizons, the rising and setting sun. Facing outwards, they are on either side of a winged scarab, which once again holds the faded sun disc in its front claws. The wings of Horus are painted in what was once a bright Egyptian blue, yellow and white.

Below the winged scarab, which represents the rising of the sun at dawn, are two recumbent lions who are guarding the rising sun. Once again, these animals face outwards and were it seems once yellow with manes of greyish appearance. The scarab and lions are flanked by a broad white stripe.

Another broad collar pattern in the usual funerary colours, breaks up the upper section of the breastplate from the lower piece, and as we look at the image on the left and right of the panel, there stand the four sons of Horus, who are there to protect the deceased's internal organs, which are held safe in four canopic jars. These are as previously mentioned the human Imsety (liver) and the jackal Duamutef (stomach) to the left, and baboon Hapi (lungs) with falcon Qebehsenuef (intestines) to the right. They are in faded colours of blue and yellow, though the red and black are more pronounced and all stand facing inwards towards the kneeling Goddess Isis wearing a blue and red alternately horizontally striped dress with red shoulder straps. Both arms are outstretched on wings painted in identical colours of the winged scarab above her. Left and right of her head are two wide green stripes and either side of these she holds a black feather of Ma'at in her outstretched hands; whilst a whitish, black eyed serpent with a pale green stripe down its front, rears up on each winged arm, facing each other. Again mirror imaging the top scarab section, there is a broad white vertical line behind the snakes and under the wings of Isis.

Below Isis is a black djed pillar topped with rams' horns; this pillar stands between five Gods on either side, painted alternately in red and black. The background for this panel of Gods is in the faded yellow as opposed to the red background of the rest of the breastplate.

Breastplate

LEG PANEL

The top of this panel depicts the deceased painted in red, the wig in blue and the Osirian false beard is attached to the chin. She lies on a lion shaped bier which is coloured black, with the central part of its body in a creamy hue which is probably a very faded yellow. Above the deceased hovers a black and faded yellow winged sun. The upper part of the wing is solid black with faded yellow/creamy colour below, and the lower feathers are black and white striped with the actual sun depicted in red in the centre of the wings.

To the right of the deceased kneels Isis dressed in red with her throne shaped head-dress also in red completing her outfit. Behind her stands a black clad God in Osirian form. To Isis's left kneels her sister Nephthys wearing a black dress with red pole and white basket head-dress; this time a red clad Osirian shaped God stands behind her.

The whole is framed in red, white, black and distressed blue squares, whilst under this frame are eight kneeling Gods in pale green and yellow with black hair, either side of a creamy djed pillar, to which is attached a snake, each facing a set of four Gods. The snakes are representing the above Goddesses Isis and Nephthys, which is evident by the crowns they are wearing.

The lower part of the panel is following the colour scheme and is in checked form down the centre with matching circles, lotus shapes, daisy shaped flower head and tear drop shapes, all in their separate horizontal sectors from top to bottom either side of the central column. This piece corresponds ornately to the other cartonnage coverings and has also retained most of its brilliance.

Leg Panel

FOOT PANEL

Finally, we come to the foot panel, which is very dark with little decoration, obviously damaged by the sands of time. A red and white checked horizontal band is bordered by a creamy line. Below this, a red panel with what looks like a white 'lower case "n" shape' (this could be depicting sandal straps on each foot), is separated by a vertical panel of black and cream stripes. There are cracks on this red foot panel with the end broken off revealing the mummy's blackened bandages underneath. The toe can just be seen through a break in the wrappings.

Foot panel

When she was taken on touring exhibitions, for safety purposes her chest and leg panels were temporarily attached. The foot case and mask were secured with "*plastazote³ wrapped in coloured acid free tissue with Japanese paper supports under weak areas⁴*".

Today she lies in pride of place in the Thacker Gallery, though unfortunately, as the name is indecipherable on the sarcophagus, she will sadly, due to ancient Egyptian beliefs, be without an afterlife. Rachel has advised me that she is currently in discussion with scientists who are intending to use chemical analysis through the glass cabinet to analyse

---

3   A versatile foam
4   These notes were taken from the Durham University Oriental Museum details

the paint pigments. This may hopefully reveal the writing of her name, therefore she will no longer be unknown, and this could also give extra information on the original colours. As we can see there is a very faded pattern on this section, with patches of colour, vertical cracks and water damage in this area. It is on this piece that the scientists will hopefully find the much-needed information.

Sarcophagus foot base

THE BRIGHTON MUMMY – DUROM.1985.61

The second human mummy displayed in the museum is that of a boy just under five foot in height, aged between eight and fifteen years old. He lived and died in Egypt c.1st Century AD during Roman rule, and is possibly from Hawara near the Faiyum, with no information as to how he met his demise.

Originally, he was bought by a dealer from an auction held by Sotherby's in July 1975, when one of the partners of the firm purchased the boy from bankrupt stock. The child was later put up for sale in a Brighton newspaper by the then owners of 'Agora Antiques'. The newspaper heading was "Wanted for a Mummy" and the selling price was in the region of £1500-2000. Amongst the interested parties was a museum, and he eventually came to the Oriental Museum in 1985.

He is displayed in a cabinet in the second of the two rooms dedicated to Egyptian artefacts, namely the Wolfson Gallery[5]. Lying supine, he is encased in Roman period wrappings, and although mummified, at the time of Roman rule the practice had waned since the earlier dynasties. On his back he has a partial shroud made from plain linen material which is adhered to the main wrappings that were wound around the torso first.

The Brighton Mummy

5   The gallery is named after the Wolfson Foundation responsible for the gallery development

Unlike former mummification wrappings, during the Graeco-Roman era the designs were very aesthetic. The intricate bandaging of the child displays this current style, which as we can see is in a diamond pattern with gilded plaster studs. This type of wrapping was common during the era, and this specimen demonstrates the beautiful and elegant features of mummification that they chose to use.

As with most mummies of the period, there would have been a facial mask, usually of board or cartonnage and painted in the features of the deceased. Rachel has been attempting to trace the face panel for further information on the child, and although the panel is missing faint contours remain.

Faint facial contours

R. J. Burwood, MA MD FRCR, of the Royal Sussex County Hospital, x-rayed the child on the 4th September 1985. The results showed his cervical spine had a *"slight flexion of deformity"*, though lateral tomography is required for further investigation. His bones are well preserved, the only skeletal deformity is an evident curvature of the spine (scoliosis). Burwood also states that from pelvic and dental tests he ages the child at around nine years old, but a qualified dentist would be more precise in aging the boy. The substance in his skull could be packing or brain residue, and there a metal, possibly gold leaf, has been placed over the mouth and nostrils.

Further tests were carried out by Dr. A. Appleby on the 2nd October 1985, who wrote to Mr. B. V. McEvedy at the Nuffield Hospital, Newcastle upon Tyne, advising of his findings. In Preston Royal Hospital, other investigations were undertaken by Dr. Edmund Tapp, the then Home Office Pathologist.

Examinations showed the skull was normal, well-formed but slightly thicker, with the cranium suggesting he was older that the suggested dental age of eight to nine years, and he was uncertain if excerebration had been carried out. There was evidence of minor deformity of the spine, which apparently had been caused post mortem along with desiccated spinal discs. There were twenty-two ribs in total, eleven either side, with the twelfth rib on the right side not fully formed. There is no skeletal disease, and the bones suggested he was fourteen to fifteen years old. Three radiologists who x-rayed him gave an age range as being under twenty-two to less than seventeen, with puberty at around thirteen to fifteen years old. Dr. Appleby also suggested that the child could be of "*negroid origin due to the skull thickness and small pelvis*". It was of his opinion that tomography tests be carried out to examine facial bones and to prove or disprove nasal brain removal. Linear tomography on the hand and wrist would also be helpful to assess the child's age along with a C.T. scan of the abdomen to ascertain if there are any organs remaining there, or if he had been eviscerated.

Taking into consideration the results from the medical fraternity, radiological evidence, dental and bone tests, they are more or less in agreement on the physical characteristics of the child and give a range of between eight to fifteen years old.

Displayed with the body was a bead net, which was sometimes placed over the torso along with amulets. The amulets shown are from other mummies; the layout has been chosen to show what may have been inserted within the child's wrappings. As we are told from the information on the amulets, this boy must have been from a well-off family, as only those with ample funds were able to afford such luxury during burials. Amongst them are Gods and Goddesses, heart scarabs, djed pillars, shabti and all other manner of talismans to help guide him through the afterlife in safety. "It must be noted that these amulets are not the posession of the child, they are a layout created from our collection that is typical of the kind of amulets that Graeco-Roman mummies may have had." – *As stated by Rachel Barclay.*

The belief is that he died as a teenager, though the reason for his demise is unknown. Sadly, there is little known about the child, including his name.

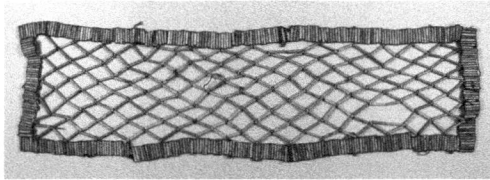

Bead net EG2424

Heart Scarab (engraved with spell to ensure heart does not betray owner at the time of judgement) EG5269

Faience Djed Pillar EG3838

Shabti EG293

THE BABY AT DURHAM – DUROM 1999.52

Death as we all know is a fact of life, but the saddest and worst for me is that of a child, especially an infant. Unlike the older boy, this child is not on display, though I was given privileged access to the baby by Rachel whilst researching for this book. Initially in the Darlington Museum, the mummy was transferred to Durham in the 1990s.

Dating to the Roman era, the baby boy is in an anthropoid form, though sadly without an Egyptian coffin. His shroud is not elaborate though he is beautifully and carefully wrapped, apparently with great tenderness. The wrappings swaddle the body using one length of material, which has been inscribed front, back and sides with hieratic script. This writing is also evident on the bandaging at the back of the neck and is possibly of a funerary nature. The relatives of the child were obviously attempting to send the baby into eternity with as much help as possible, as he is unable to speak for himself. It is hoped that one day, someone with knowledge of hieratic will be able to decipher the writing, then further information will hopefully be gained regarding the child.

Mummy of a baby is kept wrapped in tissue

Bone at side of child

Torso and lower limbs wrapped in hieratic bandaging

Back and side view of child's head with hieratic script

The whole head is blackened as we can see by the images, and this is possibly caused by the resin that was used during mummification. Regrettably the head is separate from the body and also shows damage at the back of the cranium. Through this hole the skull is just evident, and there is a crack which leads from the hole to the neck area. Although there are no facial features, this appears to be a child from an elite family who gave him a decent burial. So, maybe at one point there had been a mask which covered the face with the baby's image painted onto it, a reproduction of the child as he appeared in life.

Within the makeshift coffin in which he now lies, is what appears to be a piece of bone, possibly from the neck break. This is kept with the infant for whatever purpose it is needed in his afterlife.

Two faience necklaces made with light blue, dark blue, cream, yellow, red and green beads were with the child. They are neatly laid on a white cloth separate from the baby and along with the child are kept in storage for safety.

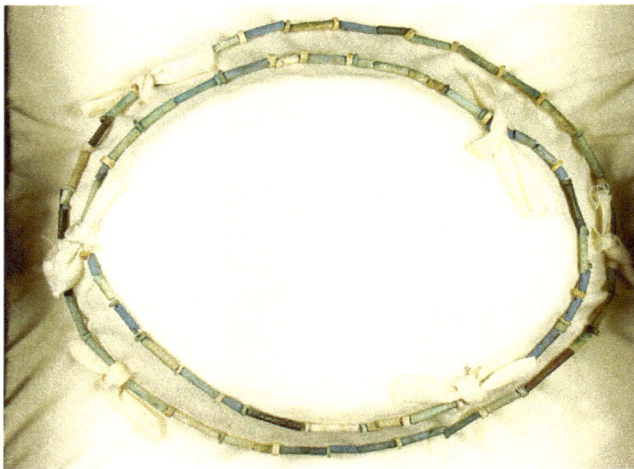

Necklace of mummy DUROM 1999.52

CHAPTER FIVE

Facial Masks

The description of the mummies would not be complete without mentioning the facial masks. These were essential in identifying the deceased in the netherworld, as the person needed to be recognised. The mummified body was completed with the addition of the mask, which covered the face and usually came down over the shoulders. As I mentioned earlier, these were decorated with the facial features of the deceased, and either basic décor was used or elaborate painting as we will see from the following.

The white plaster mask is in a simple form with very little left of this damaged item, though what remains is of interest. There are no elaborate patterns, no colour barring the eyes and from what we see, it would probably only cover the face itself.

The eyes are completely different to the usual Egyptian style. They are painted without eyebrows and are minus the thick lines that typically end at the ears. Apart from this, they do retain the 'staring' effect, which the Egyptians are extremely adept at in their art form. These eyes also appear to follow you in every direction. Below the nose is a faint depiction of the mouth.

This mask was possibly originally covered in gold leaf; the yellowing of the surface plaster in places is maybe from the glue used to adhere the gold leaf. On the inside of a separate piece is a stamp, which is difficult to read, along with two sets of legible numbers. The object is from the Roman era and was gifted to the museum by the Royal Scottish Museum.

Plaster mask DUROM.1971.183

Next, we have a full over the shoulder linen mask, which dates to the reigns of Amenhotep I to Tuthmosis I. The wig is lapis-lazuli blue with gold stripes and heavily frames a small golden face. Rachel tells me the delicate face is a "transitional form of two types of mummy mask, representing the Ba bird and traditional mask". The Egyptians believed the Ba bird represented part of a human which lived on following death. It is usually depicted as a human headed bird which can fly out of the tomb and is able to join with the person's ka (soul).

The mask looks at the reader with traditionally painted eyes and has a sensuous mouth. The shoulder piece goes down the back and is level with the front section that covers the chest and is painted with the broad collar and bordering horizontal stripes. The funerary colours of Gold, Blue and Red are again in evidence, and this person has achieved semi-divinity attested by the golden face. If the artist has captured the true features of the deceased, then in my opinion, this person was a very attractive individual.

The artefact was transferred to Durham Oriental Museum from the Wellcome Historical Medical Museum from the Wellcome collection.

Full over the shoulder mask EG733

The final mask is extremely elaborate and produced during the Ptolemaic period in cartonnage. The standard funerary colours cover the mask's surface, which again has a golden face, oval eyes complete with eyelashes, and the painting of the upper eyelid ending at the ears as do both eyebrows. The wig is decorated in various patterns in blue, black and red, with a red and white band painted in alternating vertical sections across the forehead. This wig does not appear too heavy for the face, which is in contrast to the previous mask EG733.

Across the top of the head the pattern depicts feathers which are separated at the crown by a diamond pattern in red, yellow and green. Both sides of the hair, which comes down across the shoulders and onto the chest, is of either lotus or papyrus plants with Horus next to them. The left side of the face has a large fracture from the side of the mouth to the side of the neck and across the shoulder section of the wig. From this there is white material showing from just below the ear.

Again, this object came to Durham via the Wellcome Historical Medical Museum Conservation funded by the Friends of the Oriental Museum. The previous owner of the mask was Wellcome, Sir Henry Solomon, the Wellcome Trust.

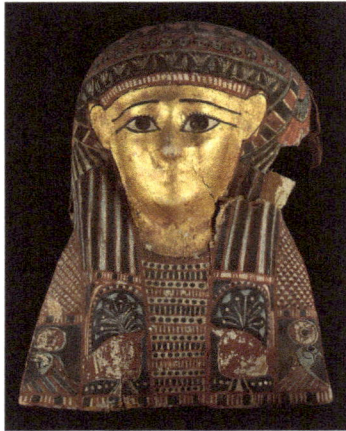

Full mask top of head diamond pattern EG732

Fracture across side of face right side of mask without facial damage

Damage to left side lotus/papyrus plants and Horus either side

CHAPTER SIX

Animals

THE JACKAL EG726

There are also numerous animals in the museum and three of which I have chosen are a jackal and two cats. The reason for this is because the Jackal is associated with Anubis, God of the dead and the cat was assigned to the Goddesses Bastet and Serket, stated in the Book of the Dead as a protector of the deceased.

Animal mummification was common, and many people requested to have their beloved animals accompany them to the next world. When x-rays and examinations were completed, in a lot of instances there have been no animal remains within the bandaging. Amongst the materials packed in to make the shape of the required pet are wood, straw, mud, linen and anything that the mortician could lay his hands on, although sometimes part of the animal was actually used. Even though there was not always a real deceased animal inside the wrapping, the mortician was very skilled in forming the shape required. Creatures were often mummified as offerings to the Gods and once again, there may or may not be the remains of the animal inside.

Hugh Percy, 10th Duke of Northumberland, owned these animals amongst other artefacts which were part of the Northumberland collection. His ancestors were great collectors of antiquities and these items were purchased from him by the museum.

Jackal EG726 and x-ray

The jackal is stunningly wrapped though the legs are not evident. The bandaging is two-tone with the top of the head, eyes, nose, mouth and back being beige. The face, front belly and chest sections are in a dark brown. The jackal's eyebrow begins in the centre of the face, rising high above the eyes, which are in the manner of typical Egyptian eye shape. As usual, the corner of the eye travels in a straight line towards the bottom of the ear, and the eye is finished off with black pupils.

Circling the neck is a narrow beige collar, and down the front of the torso is a non-descript pattern. It does appear the remains of the jackal are inside the bandages as attested by the x-ray – the shapes within do resemble bones including the vertebrae. During the mummification process, the priest wore the mask of the jackal, as this animal was associated with the God Anubis who protected the person's mummification, the cemetery and looked after the deceased in the underworld. Minus its legs, the jackal appears to be in the shape of a small walking stick.

CAT EG720

This particular cat was probably an offering to either Bastet or Sekhmet, the cat Goddesses. Wrapped in Roman style I find this mummy's facial features quite endearing. As the bandages wrap round the neck and across the top of the head, the eyes appear to be closed and drooping downwards whilst the mouth has a trace of a smile. There are, like the jackal, no legs or tail. The x-ray does seem to show a skull and spinal column, therefore some remnants of the cat could be inside the wrappings.

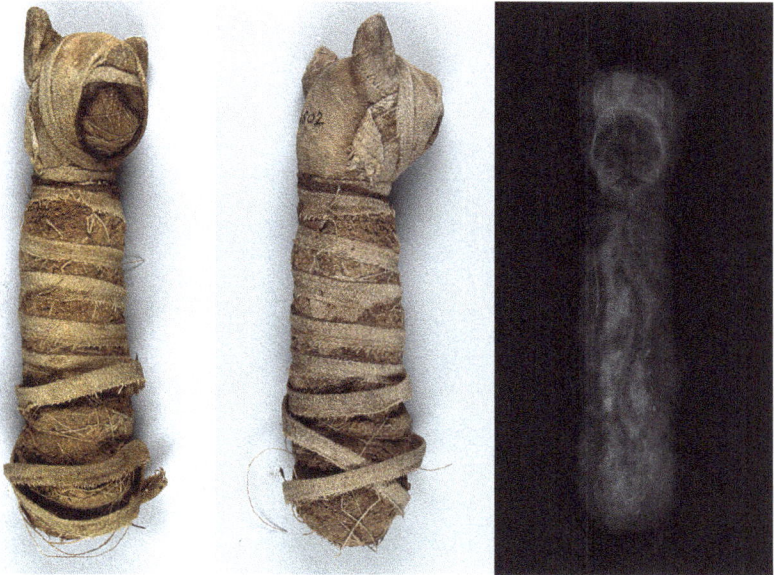

Cat EG720 and x-ray

CAT EG724

There is no evidence that the remains of the animal are inside the wrappings. Once again it is from the Roman era and wrapped in typical Roman style with a symmetrical pattern. The only section of the head which has any detail are the ears, though the whole is in very good condition. With this cat there are no x-rays to show what is inside.

Cat EG724

CHAPTER SEVEN

Birds

IBIS

Ibises were connected to the scribal God Thoth, and thousands of these mummified birds have been discovered, five hundred thousand (500,000) just at Saqqara. Many, and possibly the majority of them, were produced for offerings in temples. The following have been found to be fakes, produced using various products including fibres, linen, straw and various other materials.

Initially this item was in the Darlington Museum, and they gave it as a gift to Durham. As with many ibises' mummies, there is not a real bird internally, although it is wrapped in an ornate style, and adorned with a nemes head-dress. The inner is stuffed with various bits and pieces and maybe a few bones. The Roman diamond wrapping has this time been changed to a chevron pattern, with the feet showing a straw-like substance at the ankles. Although the pattern is different from the diamond style, the chevron pattern retains an aesthetic value. It is obvious quite a bit of care has been taken to wrap the packing, though I cannot see a resemblance to an ibis on this item.

Ibis DUROM.1999.51

Here we have another Ibis which was transferred to the Oriental Museum by the Egypt Exploration Society. Having been wrapped horizontally, with one single piece on the back wrapped diagonally, the maker decided to make the shape tubular. There is no obvious head section to let us know this is an Ibis, nor are there any feet on view. The object is only identifiable by a drawing of the bird on the front section of the wrapping. The difference in colour is due to the original photograph being taken with a different camera.

Ibis DUROM.1971.122

Now we have two falcons, one made purely from linen bandages and the other beautifully mummified in its natural form. The item made from linen has been cleverly formed in the shape of a falcon's head. Falcons represent the God Horus, protector of the pharaoh who in life was believed to be the 'living Horus'. The stand on which the object is placed, shows from the back that the item is now whole, with much of the rear section being absent. Despite this, the falcon's head is a wonderful piece of craftsmanship.

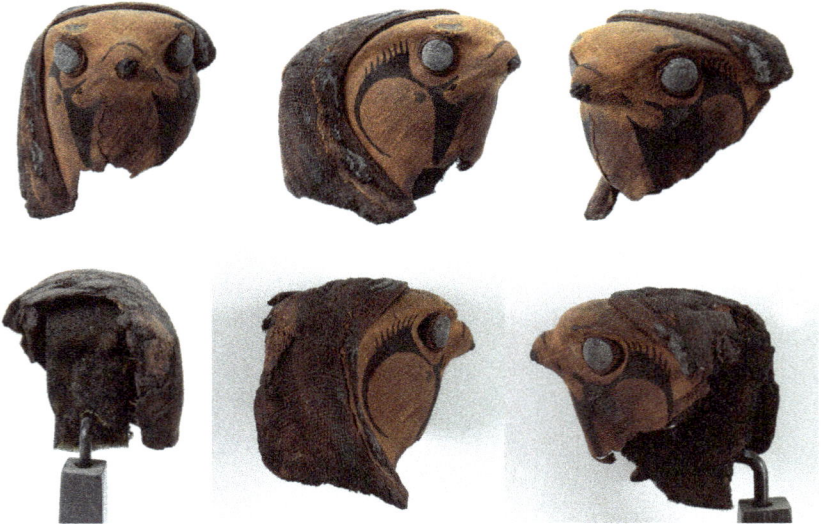

Linen Falcon Head EG5329

This falcon has been mummified in its natural form. As the picture shows, the front of the face and beak are showing, and either the bandaging has come away or it was originally made like this. One of the wing bones is uncovered as are the lower sections of the bird's legs and claws. The wrapping, which is dark and not particularly attractive, is devoid of pattern and features but despite all this, the falcon has an ethereal beauty.

Graeco-Roman Falcon EG723

Mummified reptiles have also been discovered including snakes and crocodiles, and I would be remiss in omitting the special specimen.

Inside the wrappings was expected to be a large snake, but when x-rayed there were many little ones. This item was probably an offering to the God Amun, with whom snakes were associated and whose chief temple was in Thebes, modern day Luxor. The God Atum of Heliopolis was also connected with snakes, and we know that both Thebes and Heliopolis have unearthed various remains. This bundle of snakes we are told comes from the Roman era after c.30BC.

Snakes EG719

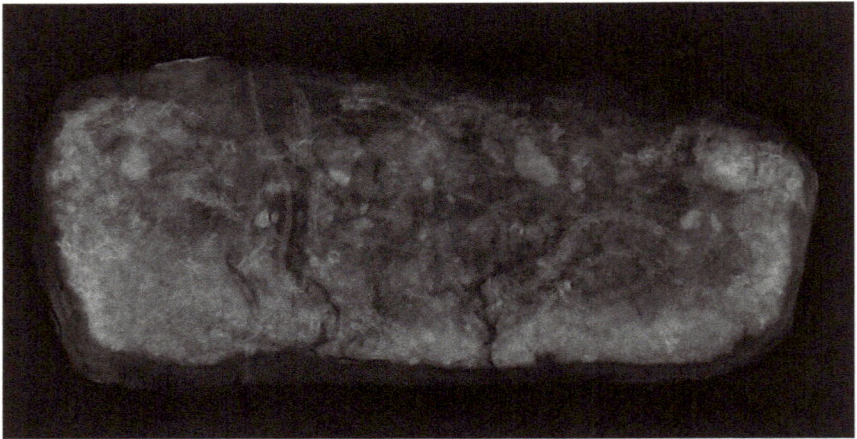

X-ray showing small snakes

CHAPTER EIGHT

Epilogue

As I have shown, there are various styles of mummification, all of which can be seen in Durham's Oriental Museum and also all over the world.

The unknown lady is a superb specimen who, by her form of mummification and coffin, appears to have been raised to elite status. Though her malformed hand and other problems tend to suggest she was born into a lower class. There are still questions needing to be answered: Who was she? What was her position in life? How old was she and was she married with children? Hopefully, with the help of scientific involvement we may in the near future know the answers to some of these questions.

As for the baby and the young boy (the Brighton mummy), there is no further information that we have for them. Unless there is someone out there with further knowledge of these children, their lives for us will remain an enigma.

Through the study of mummies, we are now aware of diseases and cures within ancient Egypt, many of which worked and others which would possibly have enhanced the sufferers' problem. With the help of modern technology, various investigations have given us an insight into the health of the people of this ancient civilisation and much of the mummification process.

The Egyptians were noted far and wide for their medicinal knowledge prior to Hippocrates; are they the true 'fathers of medicine?'

What we have learned regarding mummies is that many various forms existed, and the process was essential to their religion. Although changing over time, preservation of the body had a single purpose in mind – their quest for immortality which for many has been achieved. Let us hope in time the Unknown Lady will once again have her name spoken and that she too will enjoy eternity.

INDEX

E

Edwards, G.W., iv, 2 (*see* Peruvian mummy)

Egyptian, 1–2, 3, 5, 7, 15, 17, 18, 20, 23, 26, 28, 33, 35, 43, 44, 50, 60

    Exploration society, 55

Embalmer, 10, 13 (*see also* Mummification professionals)

Embalming, 2, 5, 7

Endoscopy, 22

Era

    Graeco-Roman, 36, 38

    Ptolemaic, 18, 20, 45

    Roman, 34, 35, 40, 44, 51, 52, 53, 57

Ethmoid, 7 (*see also* Bone)

Evisceration, 20 37

Examinations, 19, 20, 22, 37, 49

Excerebration, 20, 37 (*see also* Brain)

F

Facial, 6, 23, 24, 37, 50, 56

    Mask, 13, 16, 17, 20, 26, 27–28, 36, 42, 43–48, 51

Faience, 39

    Necklace, 42

Faiyum, 34

Falcon, 8, 29, 56, 57

Feather, 31, 45

    of Ma'at, 16, 29

Foot panel, 26, 32–34

Friends of the Oriental Museum, 46

Freund, Karl, 1 (*see also* 'The Mummy Film')

Funerary Mask, 16, 44, 45

G

Gallstones, 22

Ginger, 3 (*see also* Mummies)

Tripartite, 23, 27

Maspero, Gaston, former director Boulaq museum, 18

Mummies

Baby DUROM.1999.52, 40–42, 59

Cats, 5, 51–52 (*see also* Animals)

Falcons, 56–57 (*see also* Birds)

Ginger, 3

Ibis, 53–55 (*see also* Birds)

Jackal, 49–51, (*see also* Animals)

Natural, 2, 3, 56

Peruvian, 2

Prosthetic hand No. DUROM.1999.32.1, 18–23

Ptolemaic, 18, 20, 45

Snake, 57–58

Teenage boy No. DUROM.1985.61, 34–39, 59

Mummification, 2, 3, 4, 16, 20, 22, 23, 36, 42, 49, 50–51, 59

Origins of, 5–7

Procedure, 7–13

Professionals, 13–14

Preparation, 13

Mummy with prosthetic hand, 18–22 (*see also* Unknown Lady)

Mummiya, 1 (*see also* Bitumen)

Museum

Boulaq, 18

British, 3

Cairo, 18

Darlington library and museum, 19, 40, 53

Durham University Oriental, iii, 1, 4, 6, 18–42, 45, 46, 53, 55, 59

Historical Medical Museum Conservation, 45, 46

Manchester University museum, iii, 19

Penrith and Eden, iii, 18, 19

Royal Scottish, 44

S

Sarcophagus, 10, 33, 34
    Graphite, 10
Script
    Hieratic, 40, 41
Sekhmet, 51 (*see also* Goddesses)
Serket, 8, 49 (*see also* Goddesses)
Seth (God), 5
Shabti, 15, 38, 39
Shaman, 2
    (*see also* Peruvian mummy)
Shroud, 35, 40
Skrydstrup mummy, 2
    (*see* Denmark)
Snakes, 26–27, 30, 31, 57, 58
    (*see also* Animals and Mummies)
    Snake EG719, 58
Solomon, Sir Henry, 46
    (*see also* the Wellcome Trust)
Spells, 13, 38
    Opening of the mouth, 16
    Magical, 16
    Weighing of the Heart, 16, 26
Sphenoid, 7 (*see also* Bone)
Stomach, 7, 29 (*see also* Evisceration)
Sun disc
    Winged, 23, 27, 29
Sulphate (*see* Natron)
Sydney Thompson Chapman BA., MPhil., PhD., iii
    (*see also* Curator Penrith & Eden)

HOW TO FIND THE MUSEUM

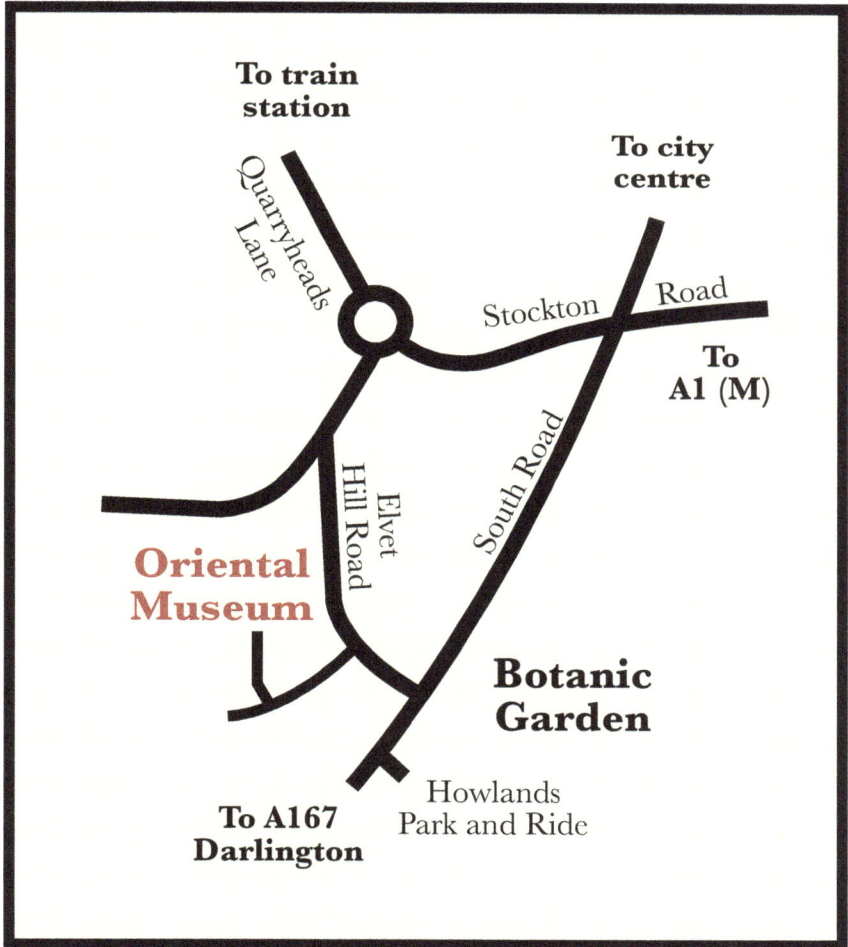